MAPWORLDS

LANDSCAPES

©1996 Franklin Watts

First American Edition 1996 by
Franklin Watts
A Division of Grolier Publishing
Sherman Turnpike
Danbury, CT 06816

Perham, Molly
    Landscapes / Molly Perham and Julian Rowe.
        p.cm.–(MapWorlds)
    Includes index.
    ISBN 0-531-14373-2
    1. Landforms—Juvenile literature. (1 Landforms.
    2.Geography.) I. Rowe, Julian. II. Title. III. Series.
GB402.P47 1995
    551.4'1—dc20   95-11947
                                                CIP.AC

Editorial planning: Serpentine Editorial
Design and typesetting: R & B Creative Services Ltd
Color origination: R&B Creative Services Ltd
Illustrations: Sallie Alane Reason

Photographic Credits:
Chris Fairclough Colour Library: 8, 14, 17, 31 (below);
Trip: cover (right), 10, 11, 18, 20-1, 22, 24, 29 (top), 31 (top);
Trip/Eye Ubiquitous: 26;
Zefa: cover (top, below and left), 6-7, 9, 12, 13, 15, 16, 19,
21, 23, 25, 27, 29 (below).

10 9 8 7 6 5 4 3 2 1
Printed in Great Britain

MAPWORLDS
LANDSCAPES

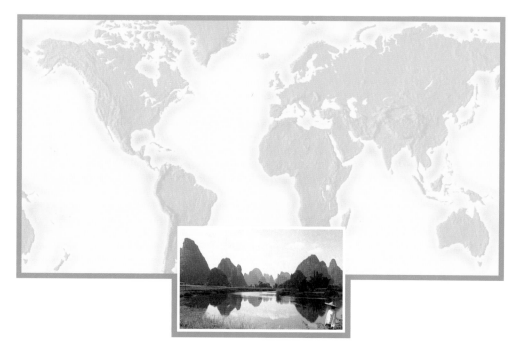

Molly Perham
and Julian Rowe

Illustrated by Sallie Alane Reason

FRANKLIN WATTS
A Division of Grolier Publishing
LONDON • NEW YORK • HONG KONG • SYDNEY
DANBURY, CONNECTICUT

CONTENTS

NORTH
AMERICA

PACIFIC
OCEAN

SOUTH
AMERICA

NORTH
ATLANTIC
OCEAN

EUROPE

ASIA

AFRICA

INDIAN
OCEAN

AUSTRALASIA

SOUTH
ATLANTIC
OCEAN

INTRODUCTION

THE FACE of the Earth is formed by natural forces. Movements of the Earth's crust push up mountain ranges. Rocks are gradually worn away by the action of the wind, ice, and water. This process is called erosion. Over a long period of time, it carves out deep valleys and leaves high peaks. Streams and glaciers pick up tiny pieces of rock and soil on the mountainside and carry them into the sea. On the way, the rock is ground into tiny grains of sand and mud.

Across most of the Earth, the rocks are covered by a thin layer of soil where plants can grow. The landscape and type of vegetation in different parts of the world depend on the type of soil and the climate. Forests are the natural vegetation of more than 40 percent of the Earth's land surface. In cold temperate regions like northern Russia and Canada, there are forests of cone-bearing, or coniferous, trees. These evergreen trees have needle-like leaves. In warm temperate regions like Northern Europe, there are forests of deciduous trees such as oak and beech, which lose their leaves in winter. Tropical rain forests are found near the Equator. Where the climate is too dry, and the soil too poor for trees to grow, there is grassland. In very dry parts of the world, there is desert.

Look at the maps and pictures in this book to find out about landscapes all around the world.

NORTH AMERICA

ATLANTIC OCEAN

SOUTH AMERICA

• A compass tells you which direction is north, south, east, and west. There is a compass like this one at the top of each map.

N
W   E
S

▷ **Hot liquid rock** below the Earth's crust wells up to the surface and creates a volcano. This is Kilauea, in central Hawaii. The active vent in Kilauea's crater is called Halemaumau. It is a vast cauldron, 1,300 feet deep; inside, the lava rises and falls.

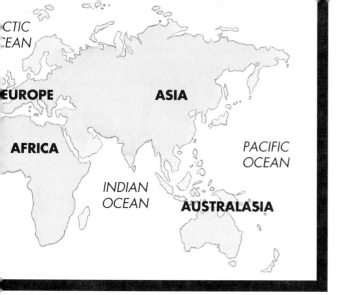

CTIC
CEAN

EUROPE   ASIA

AFRICA

PACIFIC
OCEAN

INDIAN
OCEAN

AUSTRALASIA

• As a globe shows, the Earth is round. A map is a drawing of the Earth's surface on a flat piece of paper. On each page of this book, an arrow shows which part of the globe is drawn flat on the map.

Map symbols:

These picture symbols on the maps show the types of landscape and vegetation found in selected parts of the world.

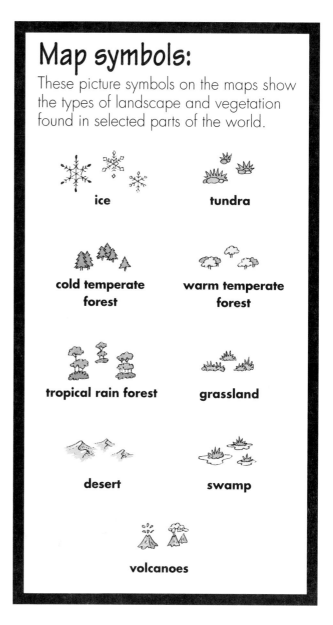

ice   **tundra**

**cold temperate
forest**   **warm temperate
forest**

tropical rain forest   **grassland**

desert   **swamp**

volcanoes

• At the bottom of each map there is a scale. The scale allows you to work out how far the real distance is between places on the map.

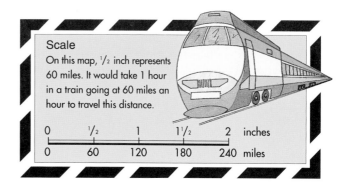

Scale
On this map, ½ inch represents 60 miles. It would take 1 hour in a train going at 60 miles an hour to travel this distance.

0	½	1	1½	2	inches
0	60	120	180	240	miles

CANADA AND THE UNITED STATES

*T*HERE ARE MANY different landscapes and climates in North America. South of the frozen wastes of the Arctic, the land is covered with coniferous forests of pines, spruces, and firs. In the center, where it is warmer and wetter, there are deciduous trees. In the southwest, some parts have less than ¾ inch of rain a year and there is hot desert.

The Rocky Mountains are part of a system of highlands called the Western Cordillera, stretching more than 3,000 miles from the Bering Strait to Mexico. The rounded slopes of the Appalachians stretch down the eastern side of North America. They are much older than the Rockies and the Coast Ranges and have been worn down by erosion. East of the Rocky Mountains lie vast grass-covered prairies, the Great Plains, now used to grow wheat and other crops.

Bering Strait

Alaska (U.S.)

▷ **The Canadian Rockies** are not as high as those in the United States, but they carry much more snow.

◁ **The Grand Canyon** has been created over a period of millions of years by the Colorado River, wearing away the rocks over which it flows. The canyon is 275 miles long, up to 1 mile deep, and up to 18 miles wide.

▽ **The San Andreas Fault** stretches 600 miles through California. A fault is where two large blocks of the Earth's outer layers slide over one another. Earthquakes are likely to happen along fault lines.

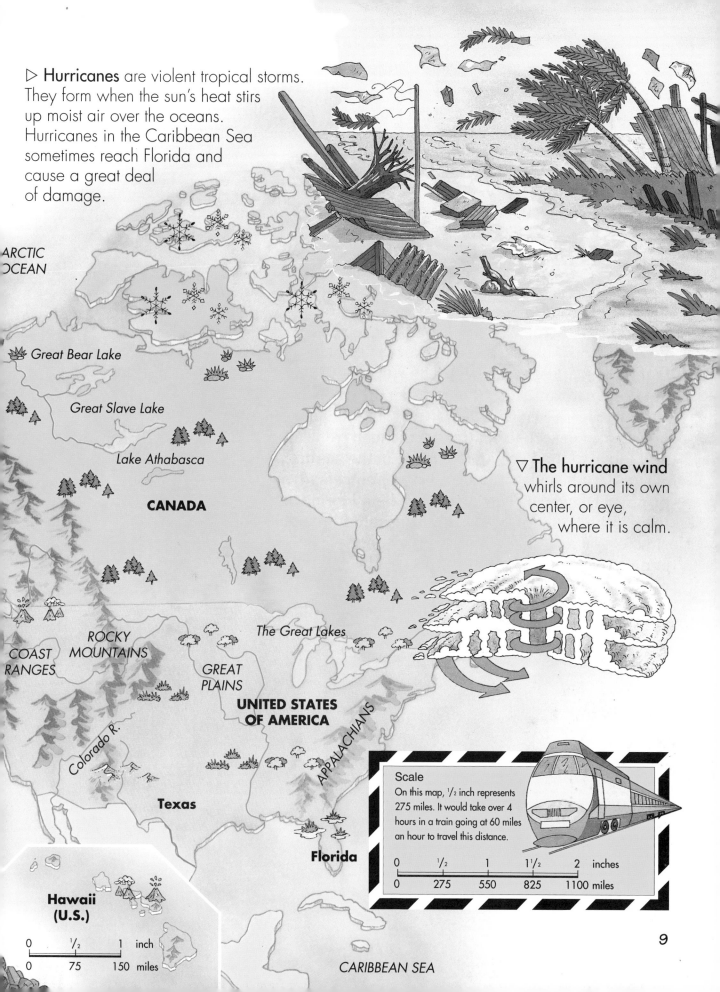

▷ **Hurricanes** are violent tropical storms. They form when the sun's heat stirs up moist air over the oceans. Hurricanes in the Caribbean Sea sometimes reach Florida and cause a great deal of damage.

ARCTIC OCEAN

Great Bear Lake

Great Slave Lake

Lake Athabasca

CANADA

▽ **The hurricane wind** whirls around its own center, or eye, where it is calm.

The Great Lakes

ROCKY MOUNTAINS

COAST RANGES

GREAT PLAINS

UNITED STATES OF AMERICA

APPALACHIANS

Colorado R.

Texas

Florida

Scale
On this map, ½ inch represents 275 miles. It would take over 4 hours in a train going at 60 miles an hour to travel this distance.

0	½	1	1½	2	inches
0	275	550	825	1100	miles

Hawaii (U.S.)

0	½	1	inch
0	75	150	miles

CARIBBEAN SEA

MEXICO, CENTRAL AMERICA,
AND THE CARIBBEAN ISLANDS

SONORAN DESERT

WESTERN SIERRA MADRE

EASTERN SIERRA MADRE

MEXICO

Popocatér (17,900

Citlalt (18,7

*T*WO MOUNTAIN RANGES, the eastern and western Sierra Madre, run down each side of Mexico. The highest peaks are Citlaltépetl and Popocatépetl – both are snow-covered volcanoes that have erupted in the past. The volcanoes rise above the high plateaus, which lie between the eastern and western Sierra Madre. The northwest of Mexico is mostly arid desert, in contrast to the lush tropical rain forest of the Yucatán Peninsula in the south.

The Caribbean Islands are a large archipelago, or group of islands, that stretches between Florida and the coast of Venezuela. They are the summits of a submerged mountain range that lies between North and South America. Many of the Caribbean Islands are of volcanic origin, and there are active volcanoes on a number of them. During the rainy season, from June to November, there are violent hurricanes.

△ **The Sonoran Desert** has many giant cacti, some as tall as 40 feet. The total annual rainfall in the desert may occur in a single day, usually as a heavy storm. Cacti are able to take in the water quickly and store it in their stems.

◁ **The rain forests** of the Yucatán Peninsula are being cleared so that local people can grow sugar cane. Felling large numbers of trees influences the climate of the whole Earth, as well as destroying the habitats of many plants and animals.

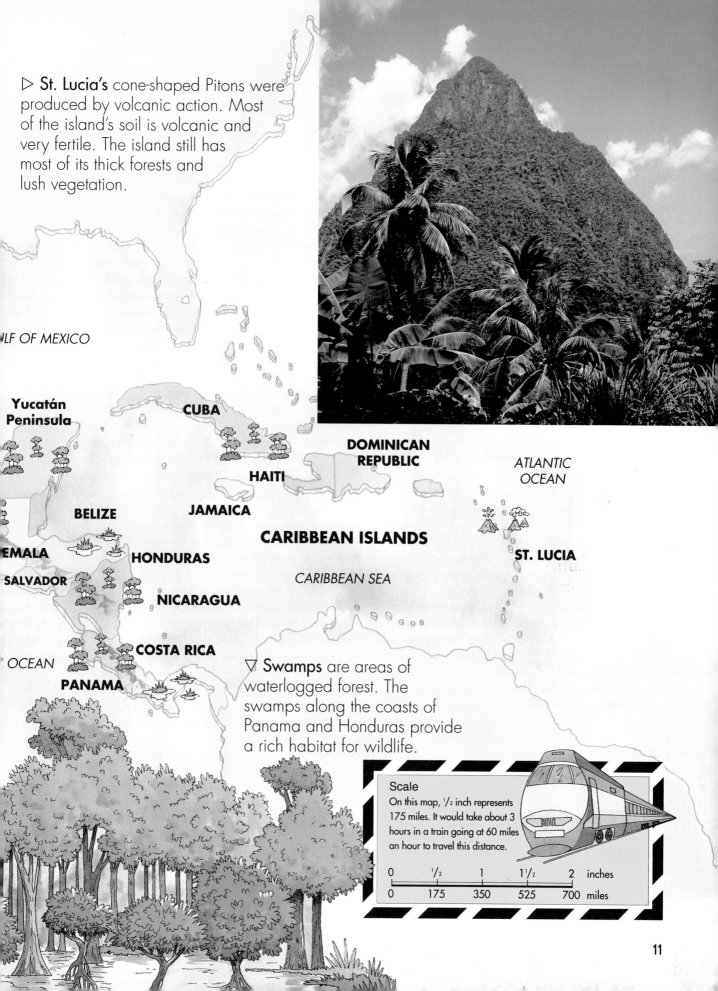

▷ **St. Lucia's** cone-shaped Pitons were produced by volcanic action. Most of the island's soil is volcanic and very fertile. The island still has most of its thick forests and lush vegetation.

GULF OF MEXICO

Yucatán Peninsula

CUBA

DOMINICAN REPUBLIC

HAITI

ATLANTIC OCEAN

JAMAICA

BELIZE

CARIBBEAN ISLANDS

GUATEMALA

HONDURAS

ST. LUCIA

EL SALVADOR

CARIBBEAN SEA

NICARAGUA

COSTA RICA

OCEAN

PANAMA

▽ **Swamps** are areas of waterlogged forest. The swamps along the coasts of Panama and Honduras provide a rich habitat for wildlife.

Scale
On this map, ½ inch represents 175 miles. It would take about 3 hours in a train going at 60 miles an hour to travel this distance.

0	½	1	1½	2	inches
0	175	350	525	700	miles

SOUTH AMERICA

THREE MAJOR KINDS of landscape make up South America. Huge expanses of rain forest cover the basins of the Amazon and Orinoco rivers. The hot, rainy climate of tropical regions near the Equator is ideal for plant growth, and thousands of different plants flourish there.

The Andes are a series of high fold mountains, with many volcanoes, that stretch the whole length of the continent from Venezuela in the north to the bleak wilderness of Tierra del Fuego in the south. Even at the Equator the peaks are so high they are covered in snow.

Paraguay and Uruguay are lands of fertile hills and plains, mostly given over to farming. Much of Argentina is covered by the third major type of landscape – the grasslands, or pampas, which are grazed by large herds of cattle.

△ **The Cordilleras of Peru** are steep mountain ridges with plateaus, called the altiplano, and valleys between them. The highest peak in Peru is Huascarán (22,205 feet), an extinct volcano. The plateaus are between 11,400 feet and 14,800 feet high.

PACIFIC OCEAN

▷ **The Atacama Desert** in northwestern Chile is the driest place on Earth. Parts of it have not had rain for more than 400 years. Rain from the east falls on the high Andes Mountains, never reaching the desert.

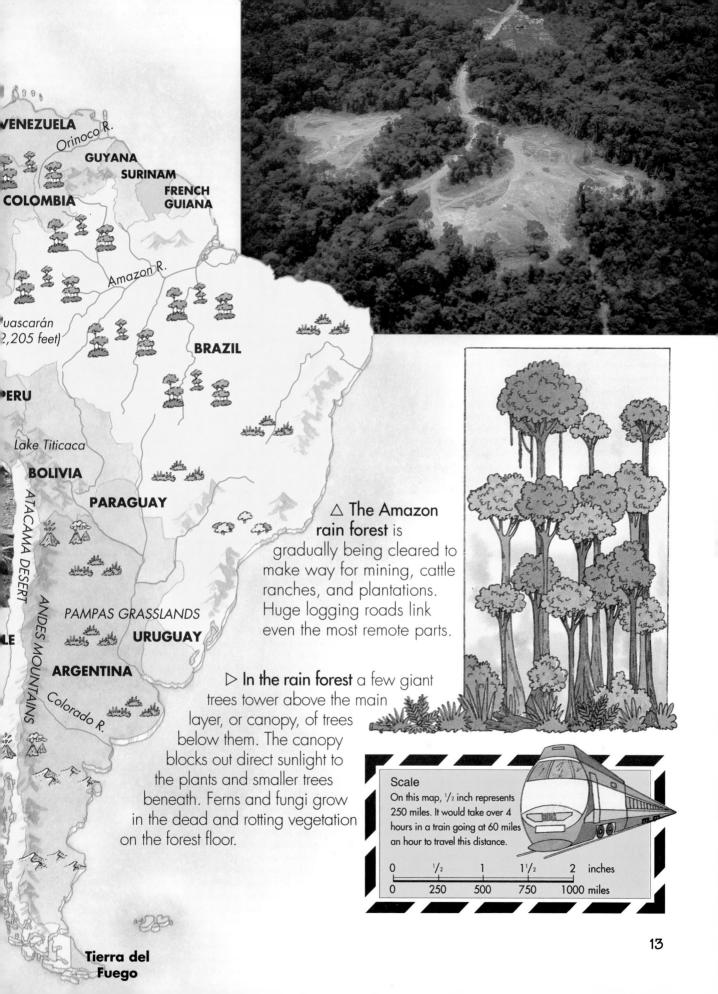

VENEZUELA
Orinoco R.
GUYANA
SURINAM
FRENCH
GUIANA
COLOMBIA
Amazon R.
uascarán
2,205 feet)
BRAZIL
PERU
Lake Titicaca
BOLIVIA
PARAGUAY
ATACAMA DESERT
PAMPAS GRASSLANDS
URUGUAY
ANDES MOUNTAINS
ARGENTINA
Colorado R.
LE

Tierra del
Fuego

△ **The Amazon rain forest** is gradually being cleared to make way for mining, cattle ranches, and plantations. Huge logging roads link even the most remote parts.

▷ **In the rain forest** a few giant trees tower above the main layer, or canopy, of trees below them. The canopy blocks out direct sunlight to the plants and smaller trees beneath. Ferns and fungi grow in the dead and rotting vegetation on the forest floor.

Scale
On this map, ¹/₂ inch represents 250 miles. It would take over 4 hours in a train going at 60 miles an hour to travel this distance.

| 0 | ¹/₂ | 1 | 1¹/₂ | 2 | inches |
| 0 | 250 | 500 | 750 | 1000 | miles |

NORTHERN EUROPE

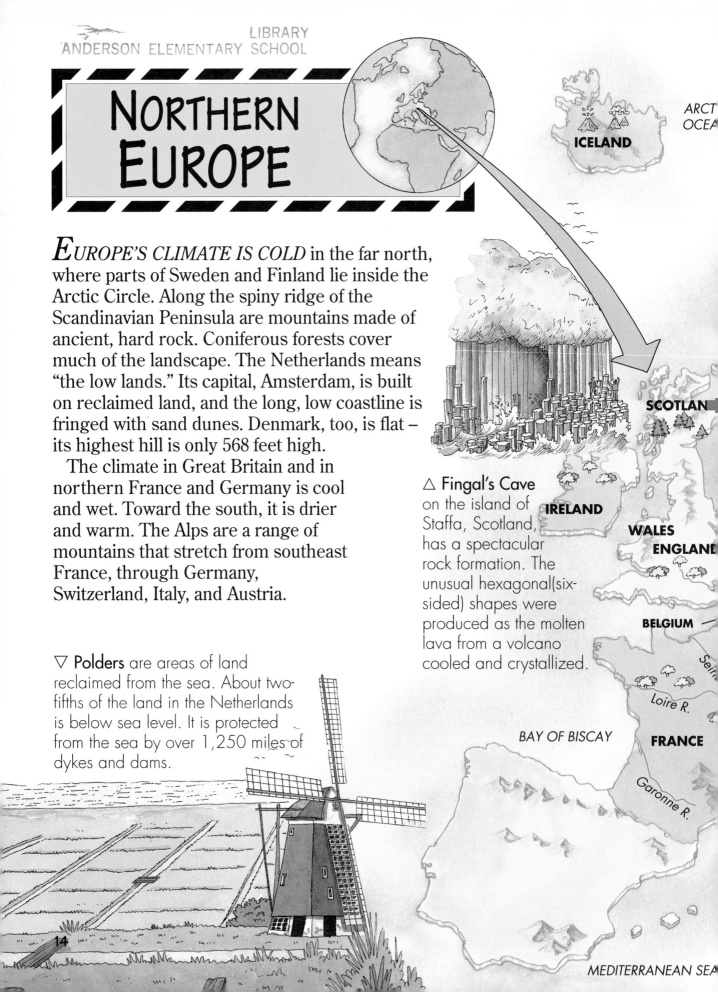

*E*UROPE'S *CLIMATE IS COLD* in the far north, where parts of Sweden and Finland lie inside the Arctic Circle. Along the spiny ridge of the Scandinavian Peninsula are mountains made of ancient, hard rock. Coniferous forests cover much of the landscape. The Netherlands means "the low lands." Its capital, Amsterdam, is built on reclaimed land, and the long, low coastline is fringed with sand dunes. Denmark, too, is flat – its highest hill is only 568 feet high.

The climate in Great Britain and in northern France and Germany is cool and wet. Toward the south, it is drier and warm. The Alps are a range of mountains that stretch from southeast France, through Germany, Switzerland, Italy, and Austria.

△ **Fingal's Cave** on the island of Staffa, Scotland, has a spectacular rock formation. The unusual hexagonal(six-sided) shapes were produced as the molten lava from a volcano cooled and crystallized.

▽ **Polders** are areas of land reclaimed from the sea. About two-fifths of the land in the Netherlands is below sea level. It is protected from the sea by over 1,250 miles of dykes and dams.

ICELAND

ARCT OCEA

SCOTLAN

IRELAND

WALES

ENGLAND

BELGIUM

Seine

Loire R.

BAY OF BISCAY

FRANCE

Garonne R.

MEDITERRANEAN SEA

14

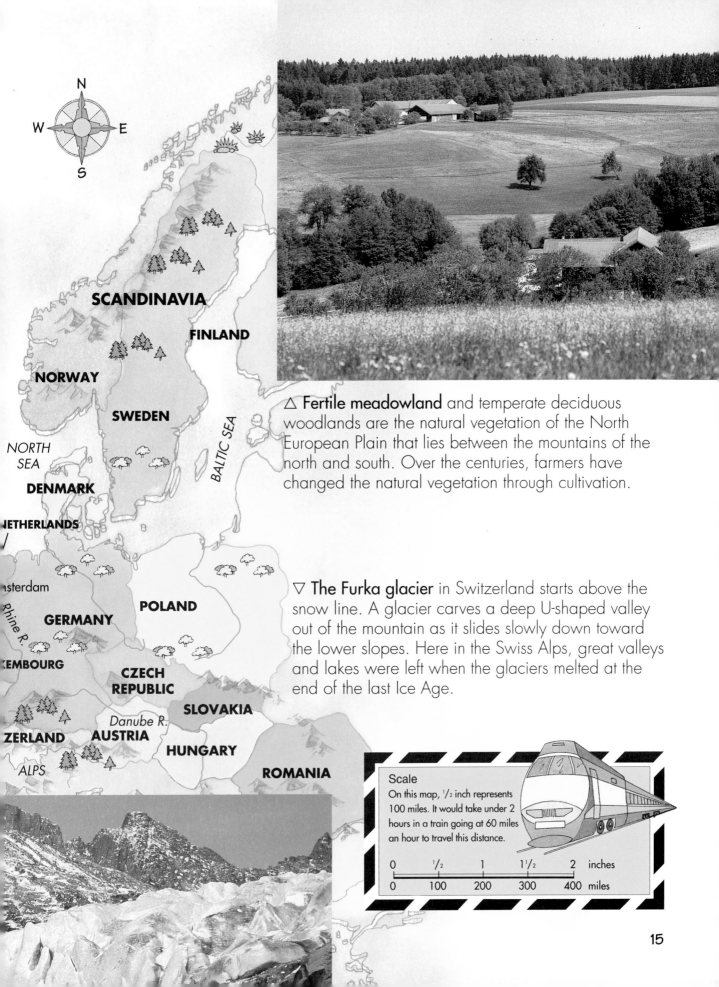

SCANDINAVIA

FINLAND

NORWAY

SWEDEN

NORTH
SEA

BALTIC SEA

DENMARK

NETHERLANDS

Amsterdam

Rhine R.

GERMANY

POLAND

LUXEMBOURG

CZECH
REPUBLIC

SLOVAKIA

Danube R.

SWITZERLAND

AUSTRIA

HUNGARY

ALPS

ROMANIA

△ **Fertile meadowland** and temperate deciduous woodlands are the natural vegetation of the North European Plain that lies between the mountains of the north and south. Over the centuries, farmers have changed the natural vegetation through cultivation.

▽ **The Furka glacier** in Switzerland starts above the snow line. A glacier carves a deep U-shaped valley out of the mountain as it slides slowly down toward the lower slopes. Here in the Swiss Alps, great valleys and lakes were left when the glaciers melted at the end of the last Ice Age.

Scale
On this map, 1/2 inch represents 100 miles. It would take under 2 hours in a train going at 60 miles an hour to travel this distance.

0	1/2	1	11/2	2	inches
0	100	200	300	400	miles

SOUTHERN EUROPE

IN THE MEDITERRANEAN region of Southern Europe summers are hot and dry, and winters warm and moist. In winter, the cold Mistral wind blows down the Rhône valley. Later, the hot and humid Sirocco blows from North Africa to Sicily and the Adriatic Sea. Over thousands of years the natural forests of this area have been cut down to make way for olive groves and other agriculture. Only a few of the original pines and evergreen cork oak trees remain. The most common vegetation is *maquis*, or small trees and drought-resistant shrubs.

Two plates of the Earth's crust collide in the Mediterranean Sea. Vesuvius, on the Italian mainland, and Stromboli under the sea north of Sicily, are active volcanoes. Many islands were formed by volcanoes that are now extinct. From the fertile plains of northern Italy, to the rocky hillsides of Greece, the Mediterranean landscape is one of the most varied in the world.

▷ **The mountains of Spain** are part of a vast range stretching across Europe and Asia to the Himalayas. They are young mountains, formed during the last 50 million years. To the north, the Cordillera Cantabrica extend into Portugal. In the south, the Sierra Nevada and Sierra de Segura lie inland from the Mediterranean coast.

▷ **When a volcano erupts,** red-hot lava (molten rock) may pour down its side, and great clouds of gas and ashes spout from the crater. Most volcanoes are caused by movements of the thick plates of rock, called tectonic plates, that make up the Earth's outer layers. Where tectonic plates collide or move apart, molten rock wells up from inside the Earth.

▽ **The island of Thera,** or Santorini, is 50 miles north of Crete. It is one of 14,000 islands in the Aegean Sea. A catastrophic earthquake in about 1470 B.C. destroyed most of Thera and its main settlement, Akrotiri. This spectacular island is now a popular tourist resort.

◁ **Water trickling** through limestone rock dissolves the rock, forming caves. Water dripping from the roof leaves deposits that grow into stalactites at a rate of 1 inch every 500 years. Water falling on the cave floor makes stalagmites in the same way.

Map labels: Po R., SLOVENIA, CROATIA, BOSNIA-HERZEGOVINA, SERBIA, MONTENEGRO, ITALY, ADRIATIC SEA, MACEDONIA, ▲Vesuvius, ALBANIA, AEGEAN SEA, ITERRANEAN SEA, GREECE, ▲Stromboli, SICILY, CRETE

Scale
On this map, ½ inch represents 100 miles. It would take under 2 hours in a train going at 60 miles an hour to travel this distance.

0	½	1	1½	2	inches
0	100	200	300	400	miles

17

AFRICA

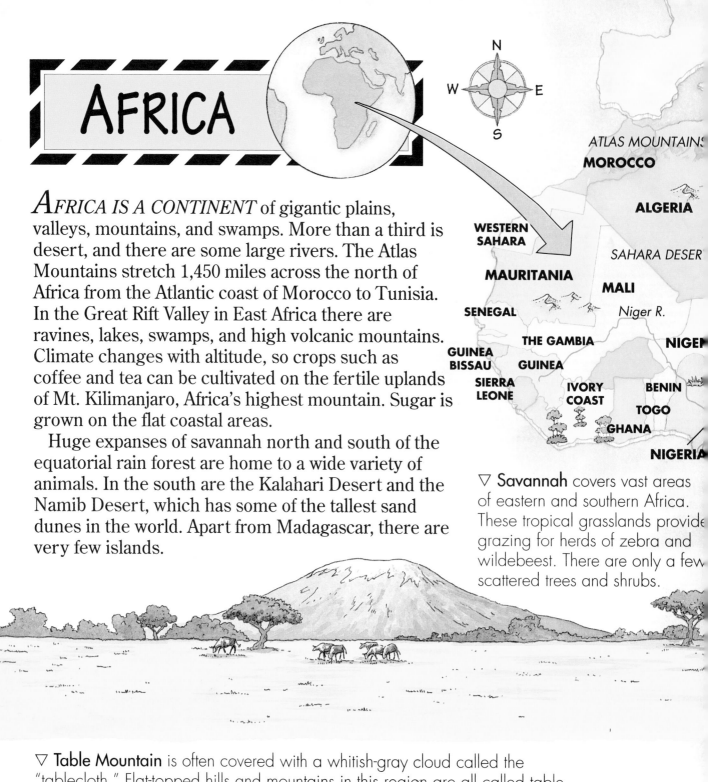

AFRICA IS A CONTINENT of gigantic plains, valleys, mountains, and swamps. More than a third is desert, and there are some large rivers. The Atlas Mountains stretch 1,450 miles across the north of Africa from the Atlantic coast of Morocco to Tunisia. In the Great Rift Valley in East Africa there are ravines, lakes, swamps, and high volcanic mountains. Climate changes with altitude, so crops such as coffee and tea can be cultivated on the fertile uplands of Mt. Kilimanjaro, Africa's highest mountain. Sugar is grown on the flat coastal areas.

Huge expanses of savannah north and south of the equatorial rain forest are home to a wide variety of animals. In the south are the Kalahari Desert and the Namib Desert, which has some of the tallest sand dunes in the world. Apart from Madagascar, there are very few islands.

ATLAS MOUNTAINS
MOROCCO
ALGERIA
WESTERN SAHARA
SAHARA DESERT
MAURITANIA
MALI
Niger R.
SENEGAL
THE GAMBIA
NIGER
GUINEA BISSAU
GUINEA
SIERRA LEONE
IVORY COAST
BENIN
TOGO
GHANA
NIGERIA

▽ **Savannah** covers vast areas of eastern and southern Africa. These tropical grasslands provide grazing for herds of zebra and wildebeest. There are only a few scattered trees and shrubs.

▽ **Table Mountain** is often covered with a whitish-gray cloud called the "tablecloth." Flat-topped hills and mountains in this region are all called table mountains. Table Mountain, overlooking Cape Town, is the most famous.

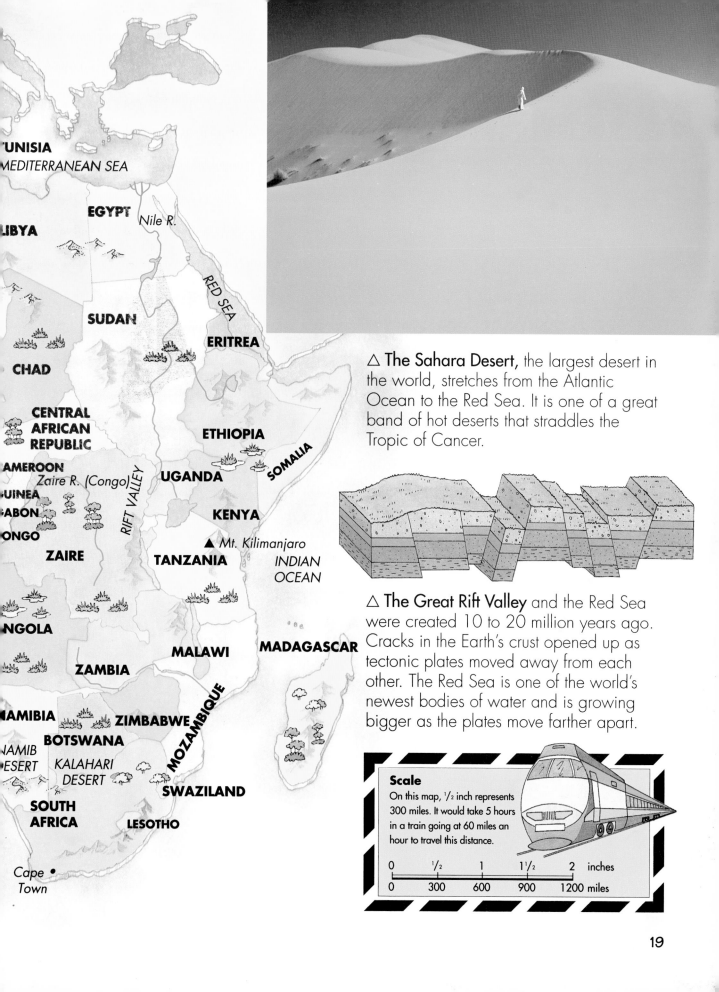

TUNISIA

MEDITERRANEAN SEA

EGYPT

Nile R.

LIBYA

RED SEA

SUDAN

ERITREA

CHAD

CENTRAL
AFRICAN
REPUBLIC

ETHIOPIA

AMEROON

Zaire R. (Congo)

UGANDA

SOMALIA

UINEA

ABON

KENYA

ONGO

RIFT VALLEY

ZAIRE

▲ Mt. Kilimanjaro

TANZANIA

INDIAN
OCEAN

NGOLA

MALAWI

MADAGASCAR

ZAMBIA

MOZAMBIQUE

AMIBIA

ZIMBABWE

BOTSWANA

NAMIB
ESERT

KALAHARI
DESERT

SWAZILAND

SOUTH
AFRICA

LESOTHO

Cape •
Town

△ **The Sahara Desert,** the largest desert in the world, stretches from the Atlantic Ocean to the Red Sea. It is one of a great band of hot deserts that straddles the Tropic of Cancer.

△ **The Great Rift Valley** and the Red Sea were created 10 to 20 million years ago. Cracks in the Earth's crust opened up as tectonic plates moved away from each other. The Red Sea is one of the world's newest bodies of water and is growing bigger as the plates move farther apart.

Scale
On this map, ¹/₂ inch represents 300 miles. It would take 5 hours in a train going at 60 miles an hour to travel this distance.

0	¹/₂	1	1¹/₂	2	inches
0	300	600	900	1200	miles

RUSSIA
AND THE FORMER SOVIET STATES

THE LANDSCAPES of this huge area range from the frozen wastes of the Arctic to the much warmer parts around the Black Sea and Caspian Sea. The Ural Mountains stretch more than 1,300 miles from north to south, forming a natural border between Europe and Asia. On the great plain to the west are coniferous forests known as taiga. These give way to grassy steppes and then the hot sandy deserts of Kazakhstan. Estonia, Latvia, and Lithuania lie on a coastal plain, where there is low-lying farmland, lakes, and swamps. The high, snow-capped Caucasus Mountains form Russia's southern border with Georgia.

Siberia, to the east of the Urals, is a vast empty wilderness. The far east is mountainous, with active volcanoes on the Kamchatka Peninsula and the island of Sakhalin.

ARCTIC OCEAN

N W E S

BARENTS SEA

BALTIC SEA

ESTONIA
LATVIA
LITHUANIA

BELARUS

UKRAINE
MOLDOVA

BLACK SEA

Volga R.

URAL MOUN

Don R.

UZBEKISTAN

CAUCASUS MOUNTAINS

CASPIAN SEA

GEORGIA

AZERBAIJAN

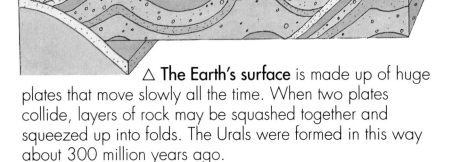

△ **The Earth's surface** is made up of huge plates that move slowly all the time. When two plates collide, layers of rock may be squashed together and squeezed up into folds. The Urals were formed in this way about 300 million years ago.

◁ **The tundra** is a cold, barren landscape on the edge of the Arctic. No trees can grow here, but the ground is covered with mosses, lichens, bushes, and small plants.

△ **In the Arctic,** ice several feet thick floats on top of the sea. Closer to shore, icebergs break off from the ice caps and glaciers on the land. Below the surface of the tundra is a frozen layer, called permafrost. The soil above thaws in summer.

RUSSIA

Yenisey R.

Siberia

Ob R.

BERING SEA

SEA OF OKHOTSK

Kamchatka Peninsula

Sakhalin

Lake Baikal

KAZAKHSTAN

Lake Balkhash

ARAL SEA

KYRGYZSTAN

TAJIKISTAN

TURKMENISTAN

▽ **Siberia** means "the sleeping land." During the long, bitterly cold winter, which lasts from September to May, the temperature often drops to minus 75°F.

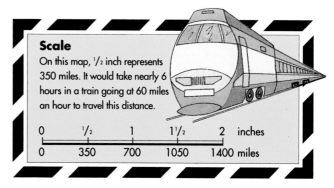

Scale

On this map, 1/2 inch represents 350 miles. It would take nearly 6 hours in a train going at 60 miles an hour to travel this distance.

0	1/2	1	1 1/2	2	inches
0	350	700	1050	1400	miles

THE MIDDLE EAST

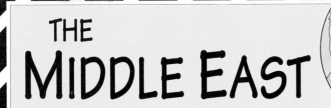

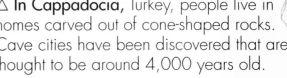

THE MIDDLE EAST is one of the hottest and driest parts of the world, with temperatures reaching 100°F to 125°F. Often there is no rain for months, or even years – and then it usually comes as a brief storm. Agriculture is possible only through irrigation, because most of the country consists of desert, dry scrub, or barren mountains.

Huge dunes of sand, some more than 900 feet high, cover the deserts of the Arabian Peninsula. The Negev in Israel is a rocky limestone plateau. In Central Turkey, Iraq, and Iran, high mountains surround arid tablelands that are covered with dry scrubland and heath. The summers are dry and hot, but winters are very cold, with frequent snowfalls. In southern Turkey and along Israel's coastal plain, the winters are mild and summers warm. Here there are evergreen forests and meadows.

△ **In Cappadocia,** Turkey, people live in homes carved out of cone-shaped rocks. Cave cities have been discovered that are thought to be around 4,000 years old.

◁ **A fertile crescent** stretches from Israel on the Mediterranean Sea through Syria and into Turkey and Iraq. Lush green crops grow on the banks of the rivers Tigris and Euphrates.

▷ **In San'a,** in the Yemen, some houses are over 1,000 years old. The are built in the traditional mud brick style, with shafts running up the middle to take fresh air to each floor.

MEDITERRANEAN SEA
LEBANON
ISRAEL
NEGEV DESERT
RED SEA
San'a

◁ **In southern Iraq**, houses have flat roofs that are used for drying crops in the sun. Families sometimes sleep out on the roof when the summer nights are very hot. The small windows help to keep the interior of the house cool.

▽ **The Negev Desert** is a dry, limestone plateau in southern Israel. When there is rain, it falls in heavy thunderstorms. The water runs quickly off the bare surface into steep-sided valleys called wadis.

Cappadocia

TURKEY

SYRIA

JORDAN

Euphrates R.

Tigris R.

IRAQ

IRAN

KUWAIT

SAUDI ARABIA

QATAR

PERSIAN GULF

UNITED ARAB EMIRATES

GULF OF OMAN

OMAN

YEMEN

GULF OF ADEN

Scale

On this map, ¹/₂ inch represents 110 miles. It would take almost 2 hours in a train going at 60 miles an hour to travel this distance.

0	¹/₂	1	1¹/₂	2	inches
0	110	220	330	440	miles

23

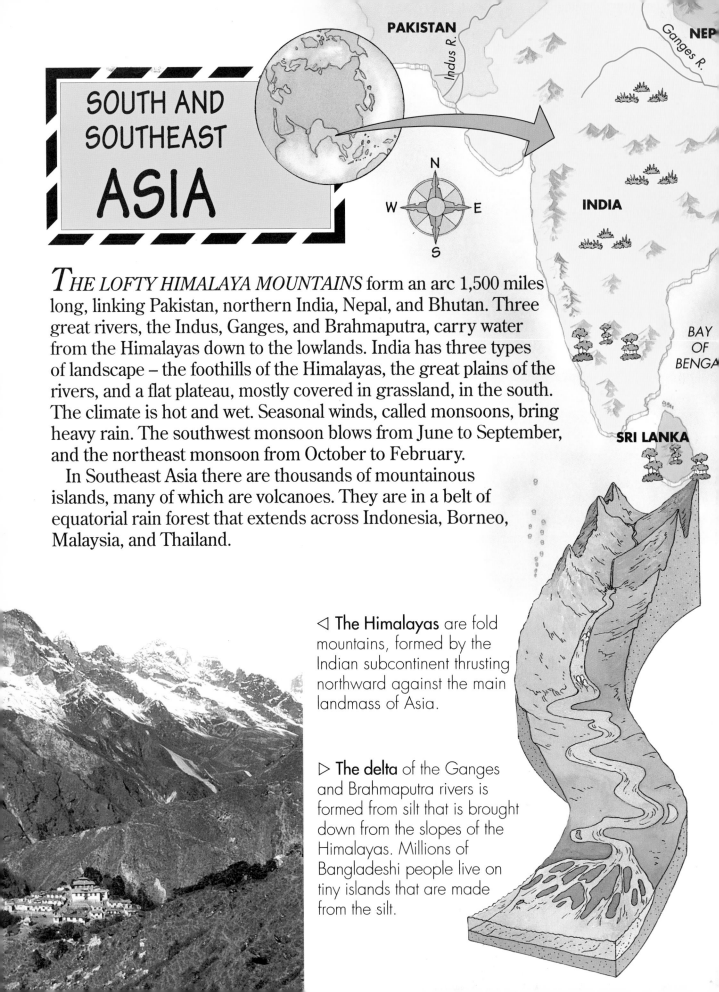

SOUTH AND SOUTHEAST ASIA

PAKISTAN

Indus R.

Ganges R.

NEP

INDIA

BAY OF BENGA

SRI LANKA

*T*HE LOFTY HIMALAYA MOUNTAINS form an arc 1,500 miles long, linking Pakistan, northern India, Nepal, and Bhutan. Three great rivers, the Indus, Ganges, and Brahmaputra, carry water from the Himalayas down to the lowlands. India has three types of landscape – the foothills of the Himalayas, the great plains of the rivers, and a flat plateau, mostly covered in grassland, in the south. The climate is hot and wet. Seasonal winds, called monsoons, bring heavy rain. The southwest monsoon blows from June to September, and the northeast monsoon from October to February.

In Southeast Asia there are thousands of mountainous islands, many of which are volcanoes. They are in a belt of equatorial rain forest that extends across Indonesia, Borneo, Malaysia, and Thailand.

◁ **The Himalayas** are fold mountains, formed by the Indian subcontinent thrusting northward against the main landmass of Asia.

▷ **The delta** of the Ganges and Brahmaputra rivers is formed from silt that is brought down from the slopes of the Himalayas. Millions of Bangladeshi people live on tiny islands that are made from the silt.

HIMALAYAS

BHUTAN

Brahmaputra R.

BANGLADESH

Irrawaddy R.

Mekong R.

VIETNAM

LAOS

MYANMAR

Chao Phraya R.

THAILAND

CAMBODIA

△ **Deciduous trees** grow at the bottom of the Himalayas. In the cooler region above is a band of coniferous forest. Above the tree line, low-growing shrubs merge into grassland and bare rock below the snow-capped peak.

▽ **In the monsoon forest** of Myanmar, some of the canopy trees, to avoid losing too much water, drop their leaves in the dry season. When the heavy, summer monsoon rains come, the plants spring to life with fresh foliage and flowers.

SOUTH CHINA SEA

PACIFIC OCEAN

MALAYSIA

Borneo

Sumatra

INDONESIA

Scale
On this map, 1/2 inch represents 150 miles. It would take 2 1/2 hours in a train going at 60 miles an hour to travel this distance.

0	1/2	1	1 1/2	2	inches
0	150	300	450	600	miles

CHINA, JAPAN, AND THE PACIFIC ISLANDS

**N
W · E
S**

MONGOLIA

GOBI DESERT

THE GREAT PLAIN of eastern China is where most Chinese people live. Water for farming is provided by the Huang He and Chiang Jiang rivers, which flow through wide valleys. The Gobi Desert, to the north, is rocky and barren. Winters are long and cold, summers short and hot. Great ranges of mountains lie along the boundaries of China.

The four main islands of Japan are mountainous and thickly forested. Most of the population lives on or around the coastline. About a third of the 200 volcanoes in the region are active, and there are frequent earthquakes. The climate is subtropical in the south and temperate in the snowy north. Each year, parts of Japan suffer damage from typhoons. The Philippines have a tropical monsoon climate, with rain for most of the year.

▽ **The Great Wall of China** was built more than 2,000 years ago to defend China from Turkish and Mongol invasions from the north-west. It now seems like part of the natural landscape and is visible from space.

Huan

CHINA

Xi Jiang R.
Guilin •
Guangxi

Tibet

◁ **The steppes** of Mongolia are one of great grassland areas of the world. In the western parts there is enough rain for grasses and shrubs to grow. In the drier east, the steppes merge into desert.

▽ **Fujiyama,** or Mount Fuji, is the highest mountain in Japan. This snow-capped wonder is a volcano which has been inactive since 1707. It is sacred to the Japanese.

NORTH KOREA

SEA OF JAPAN

▲ *Fujiyama*

JAPAN

SOUTH KOREA

PACIFIC OCEAN

YELLOW SEA

ang Jiang R.

EAST CHINA SEA

TAIWAN

△ **Guilin,** in the Guangxi province, is one of the most beautiful landscapes in China. The many tall rocks rising from the peaceful waters of the Xi Jiang river look as though they have come from an ancient Chinese painting.

SOUTH CHINA SEA

PHILIPPINES

Scale
On this map, 1/2 inch represents 140 km. It would take over 2 hours in a train going at 60 miles an hour to travel this distance.

| 0 | 1/2 | 1 | 1 1/2 | 2 | inches |
| 0 | 140 | 280 | 420 | 560 | miles |

AUSTRALASIA

AUSTRALIA IS THE WORLD's driest continent. Three-quarters of it is a vast uninhabited arid plain. Nearly all Australians live in the cities and towns along the east and southeast coast, where the climate is either temperate or subtropical. Here there are dense forests of eucalyptus trees. The northern third of the country lies in the tropics.

There are three active volcanoes and many geysers on North Island of New Zealand. West winds blowing across the Tasman Sea bring a mild, wet climate to much of the country. North Cape, at the northern tip, is subtropical. Both islands have mixed evergreen and deciduous forests. The Southern Alps dominate South Island.

Much of Papua New Guinea is covered in thick, impenetrable tropical forests, with towering mountain peaks in the center.

Northern Territory

AUSTRALIA

Lake Ey

NULLABOR PLAIN

▷ **Sandstone** is a type of layered rock. Rivers carry mud and grit out to sea, where it settles in layers on the seabed. After millions of years, under the weight of the layers above, some layers turn to stone.

△ **Ayers Rock** is a huge mass of pink sandstone in the Northern Territory of Australia. This extraordinary rock, one of the largest rock mounds in the world, is a magical place for the Aboriginal people.

28

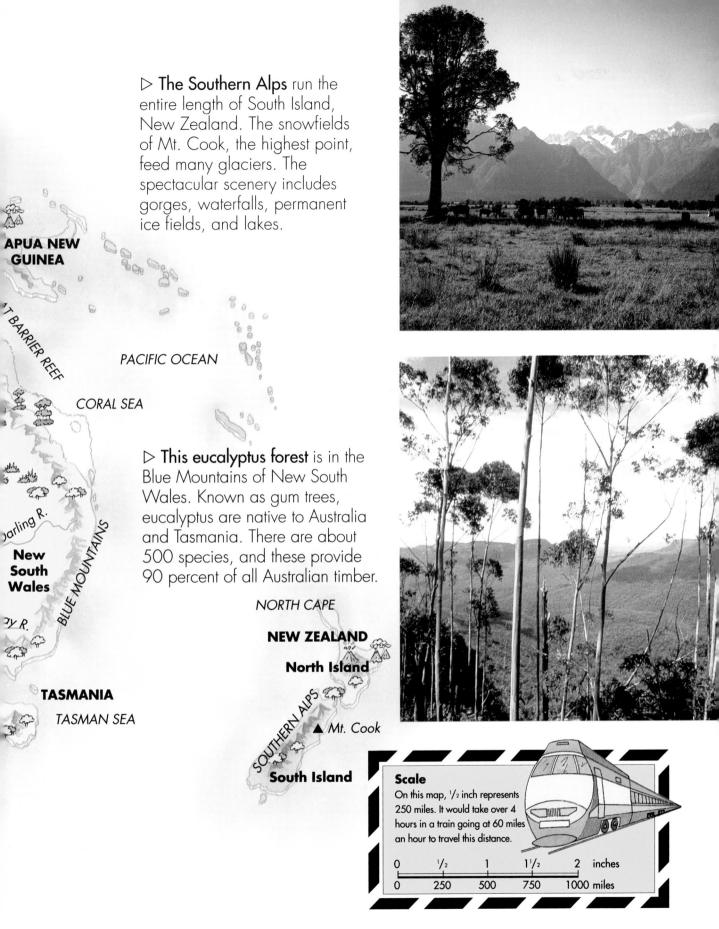

▷ **The Southern Alps** run the entire length of South Island, New Zealand. The snowfields of Mt. Cook, the highest point, feed many glaciers. The spectacular scenery includes gorges, waterfalls, permanent ice fields, and lakes.

APUA NEW
GUINEA

T BARRIER REEF

PACIFIC OCEAN

CORAL SEA

▷ **This eucalyptus forest** is in the Blue Mountains of New South Wales. Known as gum trees, eucalyptus are native to Australia and Tasmania. There are about 500 species, and these provide 90 percent of all Australian timber.

Darling R.

New
South
Wales

BLUE MOUNTAINS

y R.

TASMANIA

TASMAN SEA

NORTH CAPE

NEW ZEALAND

North Island

SOUTHERN ALPS

▲ Mt. Cook

South Island

Scale
On this map, ¹/₂ inch represents 250 miles. It would take over 4 hours in a train going at 60 miles an hour to travel this distance.

0	¹/₂	1	1¹/₂	2	inches
0	250	500	750	1000	miles

29

SAVING OUR LANDSCAPES

About one third of all the land in the world is covered with forests. Europe and North America were once richly forested, but trees were cut down as land was needed for agriculture. Today the forests in Europe are more carefully managed, and are expanding again as more trees are planted. This is just one example of saving the landscape. The amount of land available is fixed, but the population of the world is increasing. If people do not care for the land it can be eroded or changed to desert very easily.

World records
Highest point: Mt. Everest (China/Nepal): 29,028 feet.
Lowest point: The Dead Sea (Jordan/Israel): 1,286 feet below sea level.
Hottest place: Al'Aziziyah, Libya: 136°F.
Coldest place: Vostok, Antarctica: -128°F.
Driest place: Arica, Atacama Desert, Chile; rainfall 0.03 inches per year.
Wettest place: Mt. Waialeale, Hawaii: 445 inches average annual rainfall.

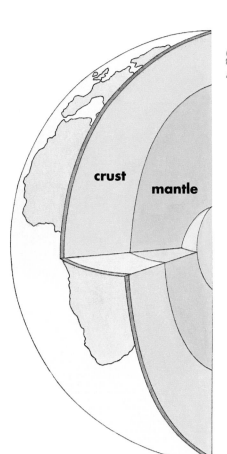

crust

mantle

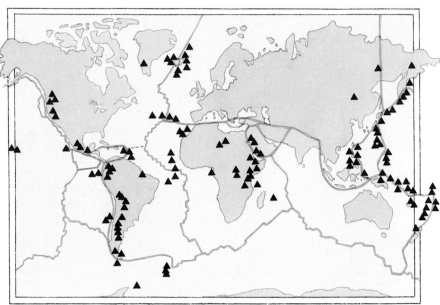

△ Plate tectonics

The Earth's outer layers, including the crust, are made up of several huge plates of rock about 60 miles thick. They float on a layer of hot, molten rock in the Earth's mantle. The plates move about 1 inch a year. During the history of the Earth, their movement has created mountain ranges and oceans. Where the plates meet, there are earthquakes and volcanoes, shown as triangles on the map above.

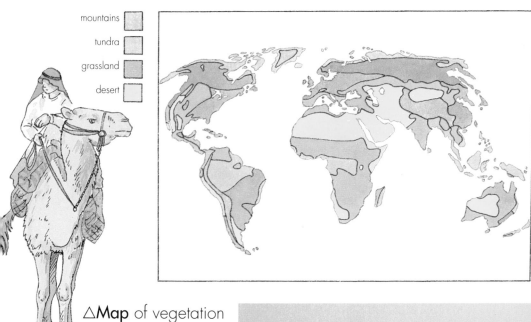

mountains ☐
tundra ☐
grassland ☐
desert ☐

cold temperate forest ☐
warm temperate forest ☐
tropical rainforest ☐

△**Map** of vegetation around the world.

▷**The world's deserts**
The expansion of deserts is called desertification. In Africa, long droughts combined with overgrazing and too much cultivation of poor soils around the edge of the Sahara is turning more land into desert. Here plants are being grown to stabilize the sand dunes at the edge of the Sahara.

◁ **The world's forests**
The destruction of forests is called deforestation. The foothills of the Himalayas have been stripped of their trees. During the monsoon season, the water is no longer absorbed by the forest and there are disastrous floods on the plains below. Here in New Zealand new trees have been planted to replace those cut down.

31

Index